Martin Luther King, Jr. Day

by Helen Frost

Consulting Editor: Gail Saunders-Smith, Ph.D.
Consultant: Alexa Sandmann, Ed.D.
Professor of Literacy
The University of Toledo
Member, National Council for the Social Studies

Pebble Books
an imprint of Capstone Press
Mankato, Minnesota

Pebble Books are published by Capstone Press
151 Good Counsel Drive, P.O. Box 669, Mankato, Minnesota 56002
http://www.capstone-press.com

Printed in the United States of America.

1 2 3 4 5 6 05 04 03 02 01 00

Library of Congress Cataloging-in-Publication Data
Frost, Helen, 1949–
Martin Luther King, Jr. Day/by Helen Frost.
p. cm.—(National holidays)
Includes bibliographical references and index.
Summary: Simple text and photographs present the work of Martin Luther King, Jr., and the celebration of his holiday.
ISBN 0-7368-0543-5
1. Martin Luther King, Jr., Day—Juvenile literature. 2. King, Martin Luther, Jr., 1929-1968—Juvenile literature. [1. Martin Luther King, Jr., Day. 2. King, Martin Luther, Jr., 1929-1968. 3. Civil rights workers. 4. Clergy. 5. Afro-Americans—Biography. 6. Holidays.] I. Title. II. Series.
E185.97.K5F77 2000
323'.092—dc21
[B] 99-049390

Note to Parents and Teachers

The National Holidays series supports national social studies standards related to understanding events that celebrate the values and principles of American democracy. This book describes and illustrates Martin Luther King, Jr. Day. The photographs support early readers in understanding the text. This book also introduces early readers to subject-specific vocabulary words, which are defined in the Words to Know section. Early readers may need assistance to read some words and to use the Table of Contents, Words to Know, Read More, Internet Sites, and Index/Word List sections of the book.

Table of Contents

January
S M T W T F S
1
2 3 4 5 6 7 8
9 10 11 12 13 14 15
16 17 18 19 20 21 22
23 24 25 26 27 28 29
30 31
ATLANTA • BIRMINGHAM • DALLAS • DETROIT • JACKSON • LITTLE ROCK • LOS ANGELES • MEMPHIS • MONTGOMERY • MIAMI • NEW ORLEANS • NEW YORK • RICHMOND • SELMA • WASHINGTON, D.C. • OSLO •
"If a man hasn't found something he will die for, he isn't fit to live."
Dr. Martin Luther King, Jr. 1929-1968 • In Memoriam

Martin Luther King, Jr. Day became a national holiday in 1986. Americans celebrate this holiday every year on the third Monday of January.

Color
Make Bob Wake up
Run, little kitten,
run!

Martin Luther King, Jr., was born in Georgia on January 15, 1929. He went to segregated schools. Segregation kept people of different races apart.

Martin grew up to be a great leader. He told people that segregation was wrong.

WE
MARCH

Martin worked hard
to change laws about
segregation. He gave
speeches and
people listened.

Our Racially
IMBALANCED
Schools
INTERNATIONAL
LADIES
WORKERS

Martin told people not to fight. He showed people how to change laws in peaceful ways.

THEY KILLED THE
DREAMER
BUT NOT HIS
DREAM

Some people did not
agree with Martin.
Someone killed him
on April 4, 1968.

WE MARCH FOR PEACE
WE MARCH FOR JUSTICE

People remember Martin's life and his ideas. Americans honor Martin by working for peace and justice.

Students learn about Martin's work. They learn how he helped to change unfair laws.

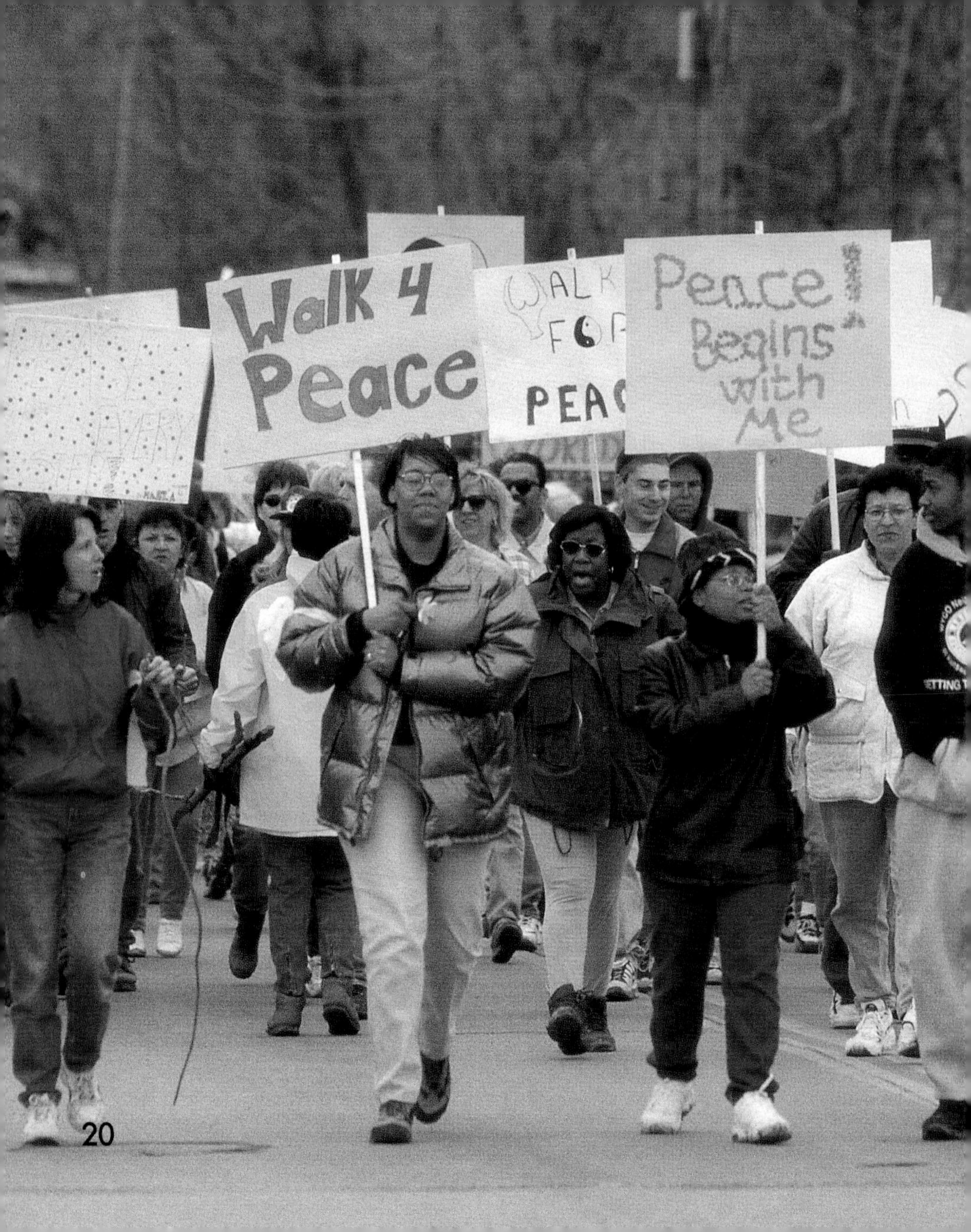
Walk 4
Peace
Peace!
Begins
with
Me

Americans of all races celebrate Martin Luther King, Jr. Day. They honor a man of peace.

Words to Know

honor—to show respect; people honor Martin Luther King, Jr., by celebrating his birthday.

justice—fair treatment or behavior

national—having to do with a country as a whole; Martin Luther King, Jr. Day is a national holiday; many schools and businesses are closed on Martin Luther King, Jr. Day.

peace—a time without war or fighting; Martin Luther King, Jr., found peaceful ways, such as nonviolent marches, to change unfair laws.

race—a group of people with common backgrounds

segregation—to separate groups of people; when Martin Luther King, Jr., was young, people often were segregated by race; different races went to different schools and ate at different restaurants.

Read More

Ansary, Mir Tamim. *Martin Luther King Jr. Day.* Holiday Histories. Des Plaines, Ill.: Heinemann Library, 1999.

McNatt, Rosemary Bray. *Martin Luther King.* New York: Greenwillow, 1995.

Schaefer, Lola M. *Martin Luther King, Jr.* Famous Americans. Mankato, Minn.: Pebble Books, 1999.

Internet Sites

Martin Luther King, Jr.
http://familyeducation.com/topic/front/0,1156,1-4644,00.html

Martin Luther King, Jr. Day on the Net
http://www.holidays.net/mlk

Seattle Times: Martin Luther King Jr.
http://www.seattletimes.com/mlk

Index/Word List

Word Count: 138
Early-Intervention Level: 13

Editorial Credits
Mari C. Schuh, editor; Heather Kindseth, cover designer; Kimberly Danger, photo researcher

Photo Credits
Archive Photos/Lass, 6 (top)
Corbis/Flip Schulke, 1, 8; Bettmann, 6 (bottom), 12, 14 (top); James L. Amos, 14 (bottom)
CNP/Archive Photos, 10
David F. Clobes, 18
Frances M. Roberts, cover, 4
J. Michael Skaggs, 16
Unicorn Stock Photos/Aneal E. Vohra, 20